New Testament Postcards

BIBLE STUDY GUIDE

From the Bible-teaching ministry of

Charles R. Swindoll

INSIGHT FOR LIVING

Charles R. Swindoll is a graduate of Dallas Theological Seminary and has served in pastorates for more than twenty-three years, including churches in Texas, New England, and California. Since 1971 he has served as senior pastor of the First Evangelical Free Church of Fullerton, California. Chuck's radio program, "Insight for Living," began in 1979. In addition to his church and radio ministries, Chuck has authored twenty-one books and numerous booklets on a variety of subjects.

Based on the outlines of Chuck's sermons, the study guide text is coauthored by Ken Gire, Jr., a graduate of Texas Christian University and Dallas Theological Seminary. The Living Insights are written by Bill Butterworth, a graduate of Florida Bible College, Dallas Theological Seminary, and Florida Atlantic University. Ken Gire, Jr. is presently the associate editor in the educational products department at Insight for Living, and Bill Butterworth is currently the director of counseling ministries.

Editor in Chief:	Cynthia Swindoll
Coauthor of Text:	Ken Gire, Jr.
Author of Living Insights:	Bill Butterworth
Editorial Assistant:	Julie Martin
Copy Supervisor:	Wendy Jones
Copy Assistants:	Jane Gillis and Delia Gomez
Director, Communications Division:	Carla Beck
Project Supervisor:	Nina Paris
Art Director:	Becky Englund
Production Artist:	Trisha Smith
Typographer:	Bob Haskins
Cover:	Painting by Rembrandt van Rijn, *The Apostle Paul*
Production Supervisor:	Deedee Snyder
Printer:	Frye and Smith

ISBN 0-8499-8287-1

Ordering Information

An album that contains six messages on three cassettes and corresponds to this study guide may be purchased through Insight for Living, Post Office Box 4444, Fullerton, California 92634. For ordering information and a current catalog, please write our office or call (714) 870-9161.

Canadian residents may obtain a catalog and ordering information through Insight for Living Ministries, Post Office Box 2510, Vancouver, British Columbia, Canada V6B 3W7, (604) 272-5811. Overseas residents should direct their correspondence to our Fullerton office.

If you wish to order by Visa or MasterCard, you are welcome to use our toll-free number, (800) 772-8888, Monday through Friday between the hours of 8:30 A.M. and 4:00 P.M., Pacific time. This number may be used anywhere in the continental United States excluding Alaska, California, and Hawaii. Orders from those areas can be made by calling our general office number, (714) 870-9161.

Table of Contents

New Testament Postcards

If it is true that the best gifts come in the smallest packages, this brief series could prove to be of the greatest benefit. Each "postcard" is a one-chapter book from the New Testament, the shortest documents preserved from the first-century canon of Scripture.

Chances are good that most Christians have never made a serious study of these little missiles of truth. That is unfortunate . . . because hidden within each is a wealth of wisdom we need today.

Have your pencil ready. We are about to embark on a journey you will not soon forget.

Chuck Swindoll

Putting Truth into Action

Knowledge apart from application falls short of God's desire for His children. Knowledge must result in change and growth. Consequently, we have constructed this Bible study guide with these purposes in mind: (1) to stimulate discovery, (2) to increase understanding, and (3) to encourage application.

At the end of each lesson is a section called ***Living Insights.*** *There you'll be given assistance in further Bible study, thoughtful interaction, and personal appropriation. This is the place where the lesson is fitted with shoe leather for your walk through the varied experiences of life.*

In wrapping up some lessons, you'll find a unit called ***Digging Deeper.*** *It will provide you with essential information and list helpful resource materials so that you can probe further into some of the issues raised in those studies.*

It's our hope that you'll discover numerous ways to use this tool. Some useful avenues we would suggest are personal meditation, joint discovery, and discussion with your spouse, family, work associates, friends, or neighbors. The study guide is also practical for church classes and, of course, as a study aid for the "Insight for Living" radio broadcast. The individual studies can usually be completed in thirty minutes. However, some are more open-ended and could be expanded for greater depth. Their use is flexible!

In order to derive the greatest benefit from this process, we suggest that you record your responses to the lessons in a notebook where writing space is plentiful. In view of the kinds of questions asked, your notebook may become a journal filled with your many discoveries and commitments. We anticipate that you will find yourself returning to it periodically for review and encouragement.

Ken Gire, Jr.
Coauthor of Text

Bill Butterworth
Author of Living Insights

New Testament
Postcards

A Postcard to Philemon

Philemon

Of Paul's thirteen letters included in the New Testament canon, Philemon is the shortest. In fact, it's really like a postcard. However, it is more than the "weather's-fine-wish-you-were-here" type of postcard that we are used to seeing. It has the personal tone of an intercessory prayer. Written from Rome, this brief appeal is addressed to a slave owner living in Colossae named Philemon. Paul appeals to this man to reinstate Onesimus, Philemon's runaway slave who had become a Christian through Paul's ministry. Between the lines of this picture postcard of forgiveness, there is a message for all of us today.

I. The Historical Background of Slavery

Paul was arrested in Jerusalem around A.D. 57, following his third missionary journey. After a number of trials spanning a two-year period, he was transported to Rome to await a hearing before Caesar (Acts 28:16–31). He was able to present the gospel to his guards and all who came to visit him while he waited under arrest in his own rented quarters (vv. 30–31). At that time, an estimated sixty million slaves inhabited the Roman Empire.

A. In Roman law. One of those sixty million slaves was Onesimus. In the earlier days of the empire, slaves living under Roman jurisdiction were offered little protection from the caprice of their masters. "The slave was absolutely at his master's disposal; for the smallest offence he might be scourged, mutilated, crucified, thrown to the wild beasts."[1] Even the enlightened Greek philosopher Aristotle referred to a slave as simply "a living instrument."[2] By the first century, however, slavery had made some significant strides.

Gaius, the Roman jurist whose *Institutes* are the most complete Roman law book that has come down to

---

1. J. B. Lightfoot, *Saint Paul's Epistles to the Colossians and to Philemon* (1879; reprint, Grand Rapids, Mich.: Zondervan Publishing House, n.d.), p. 321.

2. Aristotle *Politics* I.4.

us from near the time of Paul, states that the basic distinction in the law of persons is that all men are either free or slaves (Gaius, *Institutes*, 1.9). . . . A slave was a human being, and by Gaius's time that fact had resulted in certain protective legislation, yet even that legislation was more akin to our present laws protecting animals than human rights.[3]

Although seen as commodities, slaves were often educated, taught a trade, turned into useful members of society, and sometimes even freed.

B. In Hebrew law. Since Paul was a Hebrew, the Mosaic legislation concerning slavery should also be considered. Hebrew laws regarding slavery were exceedingly humane. According to Jeremiah 34:8–22, permanent enslavement of Hebrew men and women was strictly forbidden and denounced as a sin of such severity that it would bring about national disaster. Laws regarding the redemption of slaves were explicit, and slaves could not be kept for more than six years without their consent. According to Leviticus 25:45–46, the Hebrews were permitted to buy Gentile slaves, who then became their personal property and could be inherited by their children. However, the owner's power over the slaves was strictly limited by law: if slaves were punished in such a way as to cause permanent bodily injury, they gained their freedom as compensation (Exod. 21:26–27); if the owner's discipline was severe enough to cause the death of the slave, the owner was treated as a murderer (v. 20). Therefore, contrary to earlier Roman jurisdiction, a spirit of mercy characterized Jewish legislation regarding slavery.

A Thought to Consider

In Ephesians 6:5–9 and Colossians 3:22–4:1, Paul delineates the responsibilities of both slave and master. These two passages were written when he was imprisoned in Rome, where, most likely, Onesimus was with him. Very possibly it was their talks together that helped Paul articulate his teaching on the subject. It is interesting to note that in his teaching he made no attempt to change the existing social order. What he *did* change, however, were the relationships within that order. A new relationship between slave and master was established. This new

---

3. Francis Lyall, *Slaves, Citizens, Sons: Legal Metaphors in the Epistles* (Grand Rapids, Mich.: Academie Books, Zondervan Publishing House, 1984), p. 35. See also *The Social Context of the New Testament* by Derek Tidball (Grand Rapids, Mich.: Academie Books, Zondervan Publishing House, 1984), pp. 114–16.

relationship made the slave a better servant, for now duties were to be performed as offerings to Christ. Conversely, it also placed a higher responsibility on the master; the servant was no longer to be treated as a thing, but as a person having the dignity of a brother with equal standing before God (see Gal. 3:26–29).

II. The Background of Philemon

Two main conflicts surface in Philemon: a conflict of persons and a conflict of principles.

A. The Philemon-Onesimus conflict. After unshackling himself from servitude to Philemon, Onesimus fled to Rome—some 1,200 miles away—to find refuge. To finance his journey, Onesimus may have stolen something from Philemon (Philem. 18). At the very least, his leaving cost Philemon the price he had originally paid for the slave. So, when Onesimus ran away, he left behind not only a broken relationship but an unresolved debt.

B. The conversion-forgiveness conflict. After he was converted by Paul (Philem. 10), Onesimus, undoubtedly with Paul's help, had resolved the conflict in his own mind as to whether or not he should return to his owner. In his appeal on behalf of Onesimus, Paul addresses the conflict as to whether or not Philemon will forgive the repentant slave and accept him as a brother in the faith.

III. The Exposition of Philemon

As we turn the postcard over to read its message, our eyes immediately fall on the addresser and the addressee.

A. Greeting and salutation. This short note begins humbly and affectionately:

> Paul, a prisoner of Christ Jesus, and Timothy our brother, to Philemon our beloved brother and fellow worker, and to Apphia our sister, and to Archippus our fellow soldier, and to the church in your house: Grace to you and peace from God our Father and the Lord Jesus Christ. (vv. 1–3)

Unpretentiously, Paul refers to himself simply as *a prisoner* of Jesus Christ (v. 1a). His approach to Philemon, like that of the One whom he serves, is meek and lowly. Philemon was a convert of Paul as was Onesimus (see v. 19 and v. 10), and, similarly, is affectionately referred to as a *beloved brother* (see v. 1 and Col. 4:9). Philemon used his home for the meeting of the church where apparently Apphia—who was possibly his wife—and

Archippus—possibly his son—both assisted in the ministry. In verse 3, Paul bids his fellow worker *grace* and *peace*. Both words strengthen Paul's plea. As he appeals to the Father and the Son to show grace and peace to Philemon, so his appeal to Philemon is based on the grace and peace he should show Onesimus.

B. Commendation and request. Verses 4–7 show why Paul refers to Philemon as a *beloved brother* and a *fellow worker:*

> I thank my God always, making mention of you in my prayers, because I hear of your love, and of the faith which you have toward the Lord Jesus, and toward all the saints; and I pray that the fellowship of your faith may become effective through the knowledge of every good thing which is in you for Christ's sake. For I have come to have much joy and comfort in your love, because the hearts of the saints have been refreshed through you, brother.

Philemon's home was an oasis of refreshment to the believers who worshipped there, and the cool breezes of his *love* reached 1,200 miles across the barrenness of the empire to fill Paul with *comfort* and *joy.* Having commended Philemon, Paul begins his appeal in verses 8–10. In these verses, Paul does not pull rank on Philemon by unfolding his credentials as an apostle. Rather, he appeals to him on the basis of love:

> Therefore, though I have enough confidence in Christ to order you to do that which is proper, yet for love's sake I rather appeal to you—since I am such a person as Paul, the aged, and now also a prisoner of Christ Jesus—I appeal to you for my child, whom I have begotten in my imprisonment, Onesimus.

Onesimus—a name which grated over Philemon's tongue and left the bitter aftertaste of disloyalty and desertion. Paul mentions it here for the first time, but sweetens the word with the phrases "my child, whom I have begotten in my imprisonment." No man ever asked for fewer favors than Paul did. But in this letter he asks a favor, not so much for himself as for Onesimus. He had taken a wrong turn in his life; Paul was helping him find the way back. In verse 11, Paul reveals to Philemon the change that had taken place in Onesimus's life as a result of his new birth in Christ:

> Who formerly was useless to you, but now is useful both to you and to me.

The verses that follow provide the details for some before-and-after pictures of the slave:

And I have sent him back to you in person, that is, sending my very heart, whom I wished to keep with me, that in your behalf he might minister to me in my imprisonment for the gospel; but without your consent I did not want to do anything, that your goodness should not be as it were by compulsion, but of your own free will. For perhaps he was for this reason parted from you for a while, that you should have him back forever, no longer as a slave, but more than a slave, a beloved brother, especially to me, but how much more to you, both in the flesh and in the Lord. If then you regard me a partner, accept him as you would me. But if he has wronged you in any way, or owes you anything, charge that to my account. (vv. 12–18)

The only picture of Onesimus that Philemon had in his mind was of the *useless* Onesimus of the past—a runaway (v. 15) and a thief (v. 18). The most recent photo, however, shows a radically changed Onesimus. The picture Paul has before him is a picture of the *useful* Onesimus—a minister (v. 13) and a brother (v. 16). It is on the basis of this picture that Paul pleads with Philemon to forgive Onesimus and accept him into his home. According to a clause in Roman law known as *advocacy*, a runaway slave could return to his master and be protected if he first went to his master's friend and secured support for his cause. The friend then became an advocate, or mediator, who appealed to the slave's owner for grace and understanding. There were even some instances where the slave owner not only accepted the slave back but adopted the slave into his family. Apparently, this clause is what verses 15–16 refer to. Paul hopes Philemon will accept Onesimus with the open arms of a brother, not only in the spiritual sense—*in the Lord*—but in the physical sense as well—*in the flesh* (v. 16).

C. Promise and conclusion. As the Good Samaritan was willing to obligate himself financially for the care of the man who had fallen among robbers (Luke 10:35), so Paul was willing to put his money where his faith was in offering to repay the debt Onesimus owed Philemon:

I, Paul, am writing this with my own hand, I will repay it (lest I should mention to you that you owe to me even your own self as well). Yes, brother, let me benefit from you in the Lord; refresh my heart in Christ. (vv. 19–20)

Paul uses a subtle play on words in verse 20. The word *benefit* is the root of Onesimus's name. Essentially Paul is saying, "I am sending Onesimus to you, my friend, all debts paid. Now let me, in return, receive from you a touch of 'onesimus.'" In verses 21–24, Paul concludes his little postcard with a few closing remarks and some personal greetings from others:

> Having confidence in your obedience, I write to you, since I know that you will do even more than what I say. And at the same time also prepare me a lodging; for I hope that through your prayers I shall be given to you. Epaphras, my fellow prisoner in Christ Jesus, greets you, as do Mark, Aristarchus, Demas, Luke, my fellow workers.

Finally, as a PS, he writes verse 25:

> The grace of the Lord Jesus Christ be with your spirit.

In thumbing through the New Testament mail, we might expect to find a quick telegram from Philemon with his reply, but it is nowhere to be found. However, a church father named Ignatius, writing fifty years later in a letter to the Ephesians, addressed their wonderful minister, their bishop—his name: Onesimus. In this letter, Ignatius refers to Onesimus as the one "who formerly was useless to you, but now is useful both to you and to me." He uses the very same Greek words that appear in verse 11 of Philemon.

IV. The Application of Philemon

This ancient postcard to Philemon has a present-day postmark, with our names on the forwarding address.

A. Every Christian was once a fugitive. Every Christian was once enslaved to sin. From birth, we were all runaways. Like sheep, we had all gone our own way (Isa. 53:6).

B. Our guilt was great and our penalty was severe. The guilt was that endless gnawing in our conscience—an emptiness whimpering to be filled. The penalty was death. Like Solomon, who tried everything—wine, women, song, wisdom, laughter, building projects—we found nothing to fill the God-shaped vacuum inside us.

C. Grace allowed the right of appeal. Alone in our death-row cells, we waited for our sentence to be carried out. But, pleading to have our case appealed, Jesus stood before His Father, the Judge, and mediated on our behalf. "For there is one God, and one mediator also between God and men, the man Christ Jesus" (1 Tim. 2:5).

D. Christ paid the debt of our sin. Like Paul, Jesus said to charge the debt to His account (Col. 2:14).

E. We are accepted and adopted into God's family. As a result of Jesus' death on our behalf, we now have been accepted by the Father and adopted as sons (Gal. 4:5).

> ┌─ *A Final Postscript* ─────────────────────────
> Christianity does not help a man escape his past by running away from it—but enables him to face it through forgiveness.

Living Insights

Study One ━━━━━━━━━━━━━━━━━━━━━━━━━━━━━━━

A good way to get an overview of a book in the Bible is to map it out in a chart. A book like Philemon can be divided easily according to the paragraphs of the letter.

● After copying this chart into your notebook, come up with your own title or summary statement for each section. Then jot down any observations under each title.

	OVERVIEW OF PHILEMON				
SALUTATION	Title:	Title:	Title:	Title:	**CONCLUSION**
	Observations:	Observations:	Observations:	Observations:	
1–3	4–7	8–11	12–16	17–21	22–25

Continued on next page

7

🌿 *Living Insights*

Paul, as an apostle, was one of the most prominent authority figures in the church. Yet, his appeal to Philemon is not heavy-handed, but humble. Read through Philemon, and in the chart below, record the phrases that reflect Paul's gentle and humble tone.

The Tone of Paul's Appeal	
References	Phrases

What have you learned from the way Paul approaches Philemon in his appeal for Onesimus? As a parent, how do you appeal to your children? As a married person, how do you appeal to your mate? As a business person, how do you appeal to those under your supervision?

⛏️ *Digging Deeper*

The fact that Paul did not address the issue of slavery itself in his letter to Philemon raises an important question: Considering the abuses of slavery and its implications concerning the dignity of man, why doesn't the New Testament denounce slavery? The answer to this question has several different facets. First, since slavery was such an integral part of the ancient world, it was probably difficult for anyone writing at that time to envision an economy without it. Furthermore, had Christianity fueled the fires of a slave rebellion, the strong Roman army would have crushed the uprising with savage and tragic results, and Christianity would have been forever branded as subversive and revolutionary. In truth, Christianity could not be revolutionary in that sense, for *it is not a kingdom of this world.* It was never meant to advance by physical violence or prevail through the use of the sword (see John 18:36 and Matt. 26:51–52). It did not interfere, or attempt to interfere, with the established order. Had it done so, it would have perished in the very storm it helped to stir. It submitted to the existing powers. It raised no voice and refused no tribute to Caesar (Matt. 17:24–27, 22:17–21;

Rom. 13:1–7; 1 Tim. 2:1–4; 1 Pet. 2:13–17). The emphasis of the Christian message was aimed at individuals—not at institutions. Its life-changing power focused internally, on the heart—not externally, on laws. As the seeds planted within the hearts of these individuals took root and grew, they were, in turn, sown throughout society. Eventually and eternally, entire cultures were transformed through the pervasive nature of the truth that Christianity proclaims.

> When the Gospel taught that God had made all men and women upon earth of one family; that all alike were His sons and His daughters; that, whatever conventional distinctions human society might set up, the supreme King of Heaven refused to acknowledge any; that the slave notwithstanding his slavery was Christ's freedman, and the free notwithstanding his liberty was Christ's slave; when the Church carried out this principle by admitting the slave to her highest privileges, inviting him to kneel side by side with his master at the same holy table; when in short the Apostolic precept that 'in Christ Jesus is neither bond nor free' was not only recognised but acted upon, then slavery was doomed. Henceforward it was only a question of time.[4]

And history bears out this fact time and time again. A historical example can be seen in the life of William Wilberforce, who lived from 1759 to 1833. A Christian who served in Parliament, he led the campaign against slavery in England. After many failures, he finally obtained an act of Parliament abolishing slave trade within the British Empire in 1807. For further study, consult these sources.

- **Ancient and Medieval Slave Systems**

  Davis, David Brion. *The Problem of Slavery in Western Culture.* Ithaca, N.Y.: Cornell University Press, 1966, pp. 29–106.

  Westerman, William L. *The Slave Systems of Greek and Roman Antiquity.* Philadelphia, Pa.: American Philosophical Society, 1955.

- **The Effects of Christianity on Slavery in England**

  Latourette, Kenneth Scott. *The 19th Century in Europe: Background and the Roman Catholic Phase.* Christianity in a Revolutionary Age, vol. 1, pp. 172–82. Grand Rapids, Mich.: Zondervan Publishing House, 1969.

- **The Effects of Christianity on Slavery in the United States**

  Drake, Thomas E. *Quakers and Slavery in America.* New Haven, Conn.: Yale University Press, 1950.

  Latourette, Kenneth Scott. *The 19th Century Outside Europe: The Americas, the Pacific, Asia, and Africa.* Christianity in a Revolutionary Age, vol. 3.

---

4. Lightfoot, *Saint Paul's Epistles,* p. 325.

- **The Failure of Christianity to Speak to the Issue of Slavery in the United States**

  Scherer, Lester B. *Slavery and the Churches in Early America 1619–1819.* Grand Rapids, Mich.: William B. Eerdmans Publishing Co., 1975. In his insightful book, Scherer argues that most of the churches in America, while they did not vigorously promote slavery, nevertheless passively accommodated themselves to the economic convenience of slavery for the growing colonies. He notes some courageous exceptions, but by and large America's churches—the conscience of society—were dulled to the issue. He traces the failure of the Church to speak more aggressively on the issue all the way back to Augustine, the early fifth-century bishop of Hippo. Augustine's discussion on slavery is found in his *City of God,* book 19, chapters 14–16, and states, essentially, that the universal sinfulness entailed by the Fall required the establishment of institutions of coercion, including slavery. One wonders—if America's churches had been more conscientious, could the Civil War have been averted?

- **The Conflict of Social Responsibility versus Civil Disobedience**

  Swindoll, Charles R., and Watkins, Bill. *Relating to Others in Love: A Study of Romans 12–16.* Fullerton, Calif.: Insight for Living, 1985, pp. 17–24.

A Postcard to a Lady and Her Kids

2 John

Teeter-totters must be equally weighted or the game goes sour, as every child knows. A bigger child on one end of the wooden plank can, at will, keep the other child stranded in the air or allow the child to come crashing down to the ground. When that happens, an ankle can become sprained, a bottom bruised, or a tongue bitten. Severely out of balance, the teeter-totter not only ceases to be fun—it becomes dangerous. Similarly, when the balance between *truth* and *love* is unequally weighted in the church, it can cause serious damage. Some churches, obese with truth, bully the members that sit in their pews. Britches full of doctrine, thickly lined with Greek and Hebrew, often prove too big, and balance is upset. Plopped rotundly on the other end, love can be so gorged on a candy, gum, and soft-drink diet that it, too, can become out of balance. This seesaw effect either keeps truth teetering up in the air or sends it crashing to the ground. Some churches can be so truthful that they are often unloving; others, so loving that they are untruthful. The postcard of 2 John serves as a fulcrum to keep these two playmates in a happy balance so that neither gets hurt.

I. Introductory Questions

Although only thirteen verses long, short enough to fit on a single sheet of papyrus, this little postcard raises some important questions. Verse 1 of 2 John opens with a shroud of mystery caped around both writer and recipient: "The elder to the chosen lady and her children ..."

A. Who was "the elder"? The identity of the writer is cloaked with the simple but cryptic words *the elder.* This term comes from the Greek word *presbuteros,* which has the general meaning of "an old man." It is also used in a technical sense to designate rank or office, in which cases it is translated "elder" or "presbyter." Since John held this office while exiled on the island of Patmos, and because the letter bears the fingerprints of his language, style, and teaching, we can reasonably assume that he is the author. Why the author's name was not specifically noted is a mystery.[1] Possibly the letter came in a bundle of letters addressed to the church, making a more specific greeting unnecessary. Most likely, the anonymous yet affectionate description was sufficient identification for the reader. As a modern clergyman might sign a letter to his congregation simply

---

1. A letter similarly introduced as from "the apostles and the brethren who are elders" can be found in Acts 15:23–29.

"Your pastor," the omission of the name actually lends to its intimacy and warmth. Another reason for anonymity might be that the names were omitted to protect the writer and reader from persecution should the letter fall into the wrong hands.

B. Who was "the chosen lady"? Of equal, if not greater, mystery is the identity of the letter's recipient. Some commentators view "the chosen lady" as the church personified.[2] Although this interpretation has some merit, it appears forced in light of the more personal and individual references in verses 5, 10, and 12. The more natural rendering would be to understand *lady* in its normal sense—that is, a literal woman. There is the possibility that, like Philemon, she used her own home for the weekly church meeting. If that was not the case, she at least housed the itinerant teachers and prophets who came to minister to her congregation (v. 10).

C. What was the situation? When this letter was written, there were no completed versions of the Bible. At best, the church had the Old Testament along with a few letters and books from the New Testament. This period of fragmentary revelation necessitated a special ministry of prophets and teachers who imparted and interpreted New Covenant truth to the church. These traveling preachers were highly esteemed and quickly attained a leading position in the community.[3] Since there were no hotels as we know them today[4] and since these preachers often had few financial resources, it was necessary for the people of the church to provide food and lodging for them. It was not uncommon for such a position of privilege and responsibility to be abused by false teachers and unprincipled men. Both religious and secular writers attest to these abuses. The pagan satirists especially noted these cases:

> Lucian, the Greek writer, in his work called the *Peregrinus,* draws the picture of a man who had

2. For a defense of this interpretation, see *The Letters of John and Jude* by William Barclay (Edinburgh, Scotland: The Saint Andrew Press, 1973), pp. 151–53. Compare also the metaphor of the Church as the Bride of Christ in 2 Corinthians 11:2, Ephesians 5:22–32, and Revelation 19:7–9.

3. For a full discussion on the role of prophets, apostles, and teachers to the early church, see *The Church and the Ministry in the Early Centuries* by Thomas M. Lindsay (Minneapolis, Minn.: James Family Publishing, 1977), pp. 69–109.

4. Although public inns existed at the time Philemon was written (Luke 2:7, 10:34), they were little more than brothels. The *Mishnah,* containing four centuries of teaching by the rabbis regarding the Law, places innkeepers on the lowest scale of human degradation. Similarly, the Roman laws attest to the fact that innkeepers were untruthful, dishonest, and even oppressive. Plato refers to them as pirates. For more information, see "Inn," by W. M. Christie in *The International Standard Bible Encyclopaedia* (Grand Rapids, Mich.: William B. Eerdmans Publishing Co., 1956), vol. 3, p. 1470.

found the easiest possible way of making a living without working. He was an itinerant charlatan who lived on the fat of the land by travelling round the various communities of the Christians, and settling down wherever he liked, and living luxuriously at their expense.[5]

In *The Didachē*, or "The Teaching"[6]—the earliest book of church order—strict rules were laid down regarding itinerant prophets and teachers. A prophet was to stay only one or two days at a household. If he stayed longer than that, or if he asked for money over and above his lodging and food, he was recognized as a false prophet. Such a person was termed a *Christmonger.*[7] Apparently, the woman that John is addressing had a difficult time knowing which prophets to accept into her home and which to turn away (vv. 9–10). In her zeal to show hospitality, it seems she lost sight of discretion.

D. What is the message? Essentially, the message of 2 John is this: *Make sure your love has limits.*

Limiting Love

Rivers like the Nile and the Tigris-Euphrates were cradles of civilization. Ancient cities were established near their waters to draw from them life and livelihood. The rivers were used for drinking, irrigation, cleansing, fishing, and transportation. But when they flooded, entire cities could be wiped out. Homes were destroyed; businesses were ruined; people were drowned. If the river ever left its banks, chaos, destruction, and disease would inundate the cities. Similarly, love is a river around which a church flourishes. The banks leveed against the river of love are knowledge and discernment (Phil. 1:9). Without these restraints, love can be destructive. Opening your heart to every wind of doctrine is like opening the floodgates of spiritual destruction. A wind warning unfurls itself in Proverbs 4:23:

Watch over your heart with all diligence,
For from it flow the springs of life.

---

5. William Barclay, *The Letters of John and Jude,* p. 156.

6. For more background see "Literature, Sub-Apostolic" by Henry Cowan in *The International Standard Bible Encyclopaedia,* pp. 1898–99.

7. For a full text of the rules in *The Didachē* regarding hospitality to itinerant preachers, see *The Letters of John and Jude* by William Barclay, p. 157.

II. Expository Investigation

As this lady receives her mail from the letter carrier, she begins to read the short postcard that John has sent. Undoubtedly, John's introduction brings a smile to her face.

A. Introduction. In verses 1–4, before giving his exhortation, John greets the woman, using the example of his relationship with her as a reference point for his teaching:

> The elder to the chosen lady and her children, whom
> I love in truth; and not only I, but also all who know
> the truth. (v. 1)

His love for this lady and her children is banked on all sides "in truth." It is proper. It is pure. In verse 2, the purpose of the letter is summarized:

> For the sake of the truth which abides in us and will
> be with us forever.

He is writing "for the sake of the truth." That is what is at stake. Again, in verse 3, *truth* and *love* are linked together:

> Grace, mercy and peace will be with us, from God
> the Father and from Jesus Christ, the Son of the
> Father, in truth and love.

After the salutation, his first words are words of praise concerning the way she has raised her children:

> I was very glad to find some of your children walking
> in truth, just as we have received commandment to
> do from the Father. (v. 4)

B. Exhortation. The whole tone of John's letter is an embodiment of the very teaching he is trying to convey. In the introduction we hear how lovingly he greets her. Yet in the following verses, his voice does not fade as he instructs her in the truth:

> And now I ask you, lady, not as writing to you a new
> commandment, but the one which we have had from
> the beginning, that we love one another. And this is
> love, that we walk according to His commandments.
> This is the commandment, just as you have heard
> from the beginning, that you should walk in it.
> (vv. 5–6)

John calls the lady's attention to a clearly established commandment they "had from the beginning"—a reference to the words of Jesus in John 13:34: " 'A new commandment I give to you, that you love one another.' " Christians were to accept and accommodate one another not only to obey Christ's commandment but also to be a witness to the world: " 'By this all men will know that you are My disciples, if you have love for one another' " (13:35). However, John defines love in its true sense. Love is not a "many-splendored thing," does not "make the world go round," and is not "all we need," as contemporary lyricists would have us believe. "This is love," John says, "that we walk according to His commandments" (2 John 6).

C. Instruction. Love is the hinge on which hospitality turns to open its door.[8] But just as a door has hinges, it also has a lock. And love never opens a locked door to a wolf—even if it is dressed in sheep's clothing. This is the thrust of John's instruction:

> For many deceivers have gone out into the world, those who do not acknowledge Jesus Christ as coming in the flesh. This is the deceiver and the antichrist. Watch yourselves, that you might not lose what we have accomplished, but that you may receive a full reward. Anyone who goes too far and does not abide in the teaching of Christ, does not have God; the one who abides in the teaching, he has both the Father and the Son. (vv. 7–9)

Although a false prophet may have pulled the wool over the lady's eyes, John is not so gullible. In verse 7, he removes the prophet's white fleece to reveal the true identity of the deceiver. Despite the fact that the deceiver may speak kindly about Christ, he is really against Jesus—"antichrist"—denying that Christ came in the flesh.[9] In her zeal to be hospitable, the lady allowed a false prophet or teacher to stay under her roof and eat her food. But, in fact, she was aiding and abetting the enemy. This is why John can say that if she receives one of these deceivers into her house and embraces him with open arms by giving him a cordial greeting, then she "participates in his evil deeds" (v. 11). The world is full of deceivers, and no area is so crowded with them as the borders of religion. Most false teachers use the Bible as their base but either add to or take away from its true meaning.

8. Three key New Testament passages on hospitality—Romans 12:13, 1 Peter 4:9, and Hebrews 13:2—are all mentioned in a context of love (see Rom. 12:10, 1 Pet. 4:8, and Heb. 13:1, respectively).

9. The primary heresy that John is attacking here and also in his other letters is Gnosticism (see 1 John 2:18–27, 4:1–6, 5:5–8). Gnosticism held to the Greek philosophy of dualism. Dualism sees a contrast between spirit and matter in which spirit is viewed as good and matter as evil. The Gnostics' conclusions about Christ were influenced by this basic philosophical framework. Therefore, they believed Christ could not have come *in the flesh,* otherwise He would have been tainted with evil. Instead, they argued that the heavenly Christ only *appeared* to take on human form. This heresy was fought not only by John but by a number of the early church fathers, as traced by Reinhold Seeburg in his book *The History of Doctrines* (Grand Rapids, Mich.: Baker Book House, 1977), pp. 118–40. For more information on Gnosticism, especially how it is attacked in John's letters, consult *A Theology of the New Testament* by George Elton Ladd (Grand Rapids, Mich.: William B. Eerdmans Publishing Co., 1974), pp. 609–16.

The following fundamentals form a good checklist with which to examine the teachers that knock on your door or come into your home through the television or radio:

—Inerrancy of Scripture (2 Tim. 3:16, 2 Pet. 1:21)
—Virgin birth and deity of Christ (Isa. 7:14; Matt. 1:18–25; John 1:1, 14; 8:53–58)
—Sinless nature and life of Christ (Heb. 4:15)
—Substitutionary death of the Savior (Rom. 5:6–8, 2 Cor. 5:21)
—Effectiveness of Christ's blood to cleanse sin (Acts 20:28, Heb. 9:22, 1 John 1:7)
—Bodily resurrection of Christ from the grave (1 Cor. 15:1–11)
—Ascension of Christ and His present ministry to the believer (Eph. 4:7–10, 1 Thess. 4:13–18)
—Literal, future return of Christ to the earth (John 14:1–3, 1 Thess. 4:13–18)

A Thought to Consider

When dropping a plumb line to see if a teacher's instruction squares with the truth of Scripture, an important passage to take into consideration is Ephesians 2:20. Speaking of the Church, Paul describes it as a dwelling place of the Holy Spirit:

> Having been built upon the foundation of the apostles and prophets, Christ Jesus Himself being the corner stone.

In your investigations and discussions, always come back to the person and work of Jesus. He is the cornerstone on which a teaching will square, or over which it will stumble.

D. Conclusion. John's concluding thoughts are filled with warmth and love:

> Having many things to write to you, I do not want to do so with paper and ink; but I hope to come to you and speak face to face, that your joy may be made full. The children of your chosen sister greet you. (vv. 12–13)

A Final Application

What would you think of a physician who claimed to love mankind, yet failed to tell his patients the truth about their condition whenever the diagnosis was bleak and depressing? Would you think he really *loved* his patients? No. He would be betraying both his patients and his practice. His love would not be authentic, because it would not be backed by truth. His love would have no pedigree, but would be like a mongrel in a poodle cut. And how about your love? Is it truthful? Is it discerning? Can it spot a wolf in sheep's clothing or a mongrel in a poodle cut?

 Living Insights

Study One

What do you write to a first-century lady and her children? That question is answered for us in a careful reading of 2 John. Let's dig in.

• Continue your charting, and copy the one below in your notebook. Insert your own titles and observations. Remember to make it personal . . . be creative!

OVERVIEW OF 2 JOHN			
Title:	Title:	Title:	Title: Conclusion
Observations:	Observations:	Observations:	Observations:
1–3	4–6	7–11	12–13

 Living Insights

Study Two

What thoughts go through your mind when you visualize somebody losing balance? Pain, embarrassment, lack of control, fear? Let's look at the balance in our own lives.

• Do some self-evaluation in the following areas. (Circle one answer.)
—How would you rate your consistency in telling the truth?

Terrible   Poor   Average   Good   Excellent

Continued on next page

17

—How about your ability to demonstrate love?

Terrible   Poor   Average   Good   Excellent

—How about your use of discernment and discretion?

Terrible   Poor   Average   Good   Excellent

- Did you score lower in one area than you did in the other two? If so, how can you boost its rating over the next few days? Write out a realistic plan to aid in your improvement.
- Close in prayer. Ask God for help in this specific area. Ask Him to help you attain the godly balance that is so crucial to your spiritual life.

A Postcard of Candid Truth
3 John

How many times have you struggled in a church situation and said to yourself, "If only we could be close and committed like the first-century church!" Many read the New Testament and get the impression that the first century was the Edenic garden spot in church history. However, as we journey back in time, the travel brochures of the New Testament depict quite a different setting. There was the scorching heat of persecution, accompanied by the flies and ants of heresy that needed constant swatting. And, like sand in your bathing suit, there were always abrasive people in the church who got under your skin or rubbed you the wrong way. It was not the garden spot we like to imagine. As we turn to the postcard of 3 John, we see one of the most vivid color pictures of the New Testament church in the first century. And possibly in the glossy finish of the picture we'll catch a reflection of the church in the twentieth century.

I. Comparison with 2 John

Second John was written to a lady and her children; 3 John was written to a man and his acquaintances. The problem John addresses in his second letter regards a lady's reception of the wrong kind of travelers; in 3 John, it regards a man's rejection of the right kind of travelers. In 2 John, hospitality is misplaced; it is missing completely in 3 John. In 2 John, truth was needed to bring love back in balance; in 3 John, love was needed to bring truth back in balance. Finally, in 2 John, no personal names are mentioned, except for the Lord's; in 3 John, three specific names are listed: Gaius, Diotrephes, and Demetrius.

II. Analysis of 3 John

An outline is naturally formed around the three men whose names appear on the postcard. Gaius is the recipient of *encouragement* (vv. 1–8); Diotrephes is the subject of *criticism* (vv. 9–10); Demetrius is an example of *testimony* (vv. 11–12).

A. Encouragement of Gaius. The picture of Gaius is both warm and inviting:

> The elder to the beloved Gaius, whom I love in truth. Beloved, I pray that in all respects you may prosper and be in good health, just as your soul prospers. For I was very glad when brethren came and bore witness to your truth, that is, how you are walking in truth. I have no greater joy than this, to hear of my children walking in the truth. Beloved, you are acting faithfully in whatever you accomplish for the brethren, and especially when they are strangers;

and they bear witness to your love before the church; and you will do well to send them on their way in a manner worthy of God. For they went out for the sake of the Name, accepting nothing from the Gentiles. Therefore we ought to support such men, that we may be fellow workers with the truth. (vv. 1–8)

The elder, John, addresses a man named Gaius. Like the names Jim or John in our culture, Gaius was one of the most common names in the Roman Empire. In the New Testament alone we find three men with this name. There was Gaius the Macedonian, who, along with Aristarchus, was with Paul at the riot in Ephesus (Acts 19:29). There was Gaius of Derbe, who was delegated by his church to convey the collection for the poor to Jerusalem (Acts 20:4). There was Gaius of Corinth, who had been Paul's host, a man so hospitable he was called the host of the whole church (Rom. 16:23). He was one of the few people Paul personally baptized (1 Cor. 1:14). However, as a convert of John (3 John 3–4), this Gaius is probably not to be confused with any of the others noted in the New Testament. John was particularly fond of this man; four times he is referred to as "beloved" (vv. 1, 2, 5, 11). The greeting—"whom I love in truth"—underscores John's feelings and describes the endearing relationship he had with these people (see 2 John 1). John's first words after the greeting are in the form of a prayer, requesting "that in all respects you may prosper and be in good health, just as your soul prospers" (3 John 2). Two things are important to note in verse 2. First, notice how different John's request is in comparison to how a Gnostic teacher who taught at that time might pray. The heretical Gnostics looked down on the body and material things. They viewed them, at best, as trivial and, at worst, as evil. Second, notice how John's pattern of prayer is similar to the pattern of our Lord's life. Jesus nourished people's souls with the Sermon on the Mount, but He also nourished their bodies when He fed the five thousand. He preached that He was "the light of the world," but He also healed a man born blind. He proclaimed that He was "the resurrection and the life," but He also raised Lazarus and several others from the dead. Like Jesus, John never forgot that people have bodies as well as souls.

Prospering Proportionately

Prosperity. Every fund-raising media preacher seems to preach it. Every person in the pew seems to pursue it. Prosperity. The insatiable American dream. Once, we would have been content with a chicken in every pot. Now, we want a color TV in every room. Good health. Every best-seller list has at least one diet book in its top ten, and every video store has a new exercise tape almost monthly. Good health. Everyone seems to preach it. Everyone seems to want to pursue it. But who is preaching a prosperity of the *soul?* Who is pursuing that? John prays for his friend to prosper in all respects, both materially and physically, but also that his prosperity in those areas would be in proportion to the prosperity of his soul. How can we enjoy material prosperity and good health with the proper perspective unless our spiritual life prospers proportionately? Take a good look at your soul. Is it prospering and in good health? Or is it impoverished and anorexic?

Just as a parent delights in a child's first step, so John derives great joy from the fact that Gaius, his spiritual child, has not only taken that first step of faith but continues "walking in truth" (vv. 3–4). Like a proud father, John burst a button when the "brethren came and bore witness" regarding Gaius and how well he was internalizing his faith (v. 3). An example of how Gaius translated truth into shoe leather can be seen in verses 5–8. Gaius demonstrated faithfulness to God when he exhibited hospitality to God's children, "especially...strangers" (see Heb. 13:1–2). Within the New Testament church there were two kinds of ministers. For illustration's sake, we'll label them "pioneers" and "settlers." The pioneers were apostles, prophets, and evangelists who moved into an area, helped people come to faith in Christ, secured a core of converts that became the nucleus of a new church, and then moved on to follow the frontier. On the other hand, the settlers were local pastors and teachers who remained in their areas permanently, maturing their congregations. These congregations were the source of support and assistance for the itinerant pioneers (see 1 Cor. 9:1–14, Gal. 6:6). In verse 6, John exhorts Gaius to continue his hospitality by sending these pioneers of the faith "on their way in a manner worthy of God." They are emissaries of the King and are to be escorted in a royal manner that is "worthy of God." Because, as verse 7 indicates, they *are* worthy of God: "For they went out for the sake of the Name, accepting nothing from the Gentiles." It has never been the responsibility of nonbelievers to support Christian causes; it has always been the duty of believers, as verse 8 suggests. And that duty should be a delight (2 Cor. 9:7). To support such people, John adds, is to be "fellow workers with the truth."

B. Criticism of Diotrephes. In the same postcard, John includes a portrait of a forceful, influential man, possibly a leader in the church, who opposed John and his teaching. John's sketch of this man is darkly shadowed with charcoaled lines that smudge as our hands touch the verses:

I wrote something to the church; but Diotrephes, who loves to be first among them, does not accept what we say. For this reason, if I come, I will call attention to his deeds which he does, unjustly accusing us with wicked words; and not satisfied with this, neither does he himself receive the brethren, and he forbids those who desire to do so, and puts them out of the church. Beloved, do not imitate what is evil, but what is good. The one who does good is of God; the one who does evil has not seen God. (vv. 9–11)

As time passed, a fissure ran through the church, forming a hairline crack between the leadership of the local congregation and the itinerant ministers. Eventually, the division became so great that a fault line formed. Tremors of resentment and refused hospitality radiated from the local church's leadership. At the epicenter was a man named Diotrephes. John says this man loved to be in the center, "first among them" (v. 9a). In a quake of rejection, he shook off John's teaching (v. 9b) and tried to bury the apostle in a rock slide of sharp-edged words (v. 10a). As an aftershock, Diotrephes's refusal of hospitality extended to such extremes that he not only forbade his members to receive these visitors but expelled them from the church if they did so (v. 10).

Turning Your Life Around

John describes Diotrephes as a man with an upside-down perspective of himself—a man "who loves to be first." That little microchip description stores a world of information about his character. He runs on a me-first, look-out-for-number-one program. Type any set of variables into the computer, and the program quickly processes an automatic response. You know immediately what his relationships are like, from his social life to his sex life. He's going to be the one served, not the one serving. Like the scribes and Pharisees, who "love the place of honor at banquets" (Matt. 23:6), you can bet he'll be the one pushing to get the best seat, not the one washing anybody's feet. If you're a person "who loves to be first," Jesus has some words that will turn your upside-down life right side up: "Whoever wishes to be first among you shall be slave of all" (Mark 10:44).

C. Testimony of Demetrius. John exhorts his beloved friend not to "imitate what is evil, but what is good" (v. 11). He then turns his attention from the evil portrait of Diotrephes to the good portrait of Demetrius in verse 12:

> Demetrius has received a good testimony from everyone, and from the truth itself; and we also bear witness, and you know that our witness is true.

Demetrius probably delivered this short letter to Gaius. To introduce the mail carrier, John lists three impressive references for the messenger's accreditation. First, he received a good testimony universally—"from everyone." Second, he received a good testimony "from the truth itself." That is, if truth could talk, it would testify that his life lined up with its teaching and practice. Third, he received a good testimony from the apostle and his close circle of friends—"and we also bear witness."

D. Final postscript. In spite of the disruptions from Diotrephes, John is eager to visit them, to wish them peace, and to send greetings from other friends:

I had many things to write to you, but I am not willing to write them to you with pen and ink; but I hope to see you shortly, and we shall speak face to face. Peace be to you. The friends greet you. Greet the friends by name. (vv. 13–14)

Demetrius, Diotrephes, and Gaius represent the peaks and valleys in the early Church's landscape. As mountains cannot exist without valleys, so it seems that churches, whether first-century or twentieth-century, cannot exist without at least some low points. Be realistic in understanding that your church will have its Diotrepheses. But be encouraged that there will be Demetriuses and Gaiuses at the pinnacle—reaching for the heavens.

Living Insights

Study One ▬▬▬▬▬▬▬▬▬▬▬▬▬▬▬▬▬▬▬▬▬▬▬

Are you getting the knack of charting? Many Bible students feel the chart is the most valuable tool in inductive Bible study.

- Transfer this chart into your notebook. Create a title for each section and then list your observations about each. Give it a personal touch . . . make it unmistakably yours!

	OVERVIEW OF 3 JOHN			
SALUTATION	Title:	Title:	Title:	CONCLUSION
	Observations:	Observations:	Observations:	
1	2–8	9–11	12–13	14

Living Insights

Third John can be easily outlined around the three characters addressed in the letter. Let's bring all of them together for some personal application.

—Gaius was faithful and hospitable. How can *you* demonstrate some of his positive traits this week? List three ways.

—Diotrephes was rebuked for being prideful, disruptive, inhospitable, and coercive. Jot down some ways you can avoid falling into these traps.

—Demetrius was praised for his good *testimony.* Would you be characterized in the same way? Write down two or three areas of your life that need work.

The Acts of the Apostates
Jude 1–4

Shakespeare said it in his play *As You Like It:*
> All the world's a stage,
> And all the men and women merely players. . . .[1]

In the theater of world events, Christians have the VIP privilege of going backstage before the curtain call of the future apocalyptic drama. Although we don't know specifically when the curtain will rise on the end times, the Word of God provides us with a playbill describing the cast and how act 1 will open. In Matthew 24:11, Jesus reveals the cast that will act out the final scenes: " 'Many false prophets will arise, and will mislead many.' " Paul sets the first scene in 1 Timothy 4:1: "In later times some will fall away from the faith." In 2 Timothy 4:3–4, he adds: "The time will come when they will not endure sound doctrine . . . and will turn away their ears from the truth." Again, in 2 Thessalonians 2:3, Paul warns: "Let no one in any way deceive you, for it will not come unless the apostasy comes first." Like the sounds of the instruments being warmed up in the orchestra pit, these verses overlap each other in announcing that the opening act leading to the climactic Battle of Armageddon will be apostasy. In a word, that's what this postcard from Jude is all about—*apostasy.*

I. The Author and the Audience
The first two verses of Jude introduce us to the author and his audience:
> Jude, a bond-servant of Jesus Christ, and brother of James, to those who are the called, beloved in God the Father, and kept for Jesus Christ: May mercy and peace and love be multiplied to you. (vv. 1–2)

The author identifies himself as Jude, "a bond-servant of Jesus Christ, and brother of James." Most likely, he is the half brother of Jesus, the son of Mary and Joseph (see Matt. 13:55 and Mark 6:3). Few things tell more about a man than the way he speaks of himself. Like his brother James, Jude describes himself simply as a "bond-servant" (James 1:1). In other words, Jude regards himself as having only one distinction in life—to be forever at the disposal of Jesus, his Master. The audience to whom this servant is writing is described as "called," "beloved," and "kept." The call of God is a call to be loved and kept securely in the love of Jesus Christ (see Rom. 8:30–39). This letter was specifically addressed to the born-again believers of Jude's day, but it applies to Christians for all time.

---

1. William Shakespeare in *Bartlett's Familiar Quotations,* 14th ed. (Boston, Mass.: Little, Brown and Co., 1968), p. 248.

II. The Admonition

Jude's original intention was to write a treatise on the subject of "our common salvation" (v. 3). But a boulder on his mental track caused him to abruptly switch subjects. That boulder weighed heavily on his mind, because if not removed, it would derail the faith of his beloved readers:

> Beloved, while I was making every effort to write you about our common salvation, I felt the necessity to write to you appealing that you contend earnestly for the faith which was once for all delivered to the saints.

The theme of this letter is found in the admonition to "contend earnestly for the faith." The Greek word for "contend" is *epagonizesthai*. It means "to fight" or "to struggle" intensely. Look carefully at the Greek word, and you'll see the root from which it's taken. We get our word *agonize* from it. The picture is one of a wrestling match with a formidable opponent in an ancient gymnasium, thick and humid with the smell of sweat.

Some Personal Application

Topping the agendas of many church board meetings is the issue of making churches more comfortable places for their members. A new air-conditioning system . . . bigger class-rooms . . . cushions for the pews. The list goes on and on. Topping Jude's agenda is an admonition to sweat—"Contend earnestly for the faith." Don't let someone take away the nucleus of your faith without a struggle. It's worth fighting for, so don't be afraid to get on the canvas and wrestle for it. But if your focus is on comfortable pews and thermostat settings, are you really going to want to break into a sweat and "contend earnestly for the faith"?

"The faith" Jude admonishes us to contend for is the body of truth contained in the Scriptures—the truth that not only affects our liturgy but our lifestyle. It was faith that was delivered "once for all." The core of the Christian faith is a solid nucleus of truth. It isn't in a state of flux. Unlike modeling clay, it can't be molded around each new generation's lifestyles. "The faith" is firmly structured around the good news delivered *once* at the cross—and *for all*. Notice, too, that the faith is not delivered to a privileged few on God's list. It isn't given to the clergy; it's given "to the saints."

Truth is not esoteric—for a few. It's egalitarian—for all. The New Testament wasn't written in classical Greek—for the elite. It was written in *Koinē* Greek—for the person on the street.[2]

III. The Apostates

The reason we should "contend earnestly for the faith" is given in verse 4:

> For certain persons have crept in unnoticed, those who were long beforehand marked out for this condemnation, ungodly persons who turn the grace of our God into licentiousness and deny our only Master and Lord, Jesus Christ.

Apostasy is a falling-away from the faith. The picture is not one of drifting away but of defection and desertion. In classical Greek literature the word *apostasy* is used of rebels who defect from a cause. It is also used in the phrase "bill of divorce," where the word *divorce* is a translation of the Greek word *apostasia.*[3] Apostates were people who opposed the mainstream teaching of the Christian faith. They did not harbor doubts in their minds but full-sailed defiance in their hearts. And everywhere these defiant men went, division and dissension followed. Unlike the apostles, who announced their coming to the churches and had a very high profile, the apostates "crept in unnoticed." This phrase comes from the Greek word *pareiseduō,* meaning "to slip in stealthily." Barclay, in his commentary on Jude, vividly relates how this word was used in biblical times:

> It is used of the specious and seductive words of a clever pleader seeping gradually into the minds of a judge and jury; it is used of an outlaw slipping secretly back into the country from which he has been expelled; it is used of the slow and subtle entry of innovations into the life of state, which in the end undermine and break down the ancestral laws. It always indicates a secret, stealthy, and subtle insinuation of something evil into a society or a situation.[4]

2. *Koinē* (lit. common) Greek was the language of everyday life. The difference between classical Greek and *Koinē* approximates the difference between the King James Version of the Bible and a modern paraphrase like The Living Bible.

3. Henry George Liddell and Robert Scott, *A Greek-English Lexicon* (Oxford, England: Clarendon Press, 1973), p. 218.

4. William Barclay, *The Letters of John and Jude* (Edinburgh, Scotland: The Saint Andrew Press, 1973), p. 211.

In classical Greek literature, the word referred to slipping poison into someone's glass.[5] As poison dropped furtively into a silver chalice, these men surreptitiously penetrated the church. And their effect was lethal, striking at the very core of Christian truth. Jude describes these "ungodly persons" in two ways. First, they "turn the grace of our God into licentiousness." Second, they "deny our only Master and Lord, Jesus Christ." It is easy to take grace for granted. These apostates, however, went several steps further. They twisted it and turned it into an opportunity to satisfy their own sensual appetites.[6] The word *turn* in verse 4 means "to transpose" or "change the place of." It is used to describe the altering of a conclusion, or the changing of a person's name, mind, or loyalties. In secular literature written at the time of the New Testament, this word is used to describe Dionysius of Heracleia, who deserted the Stoics for the Epicureans. He is termed "the turncoat"—the same word that is found in Jude 4.[7] Reversing grace into a cloak for evil, the "ravenous wolves" (see Matt. 7:15) broke the leash of Christ's authority, running wild and, apparently, unchecked. The words of Edmund Burke serve to underscore the urgency of the situation:

> The only thing necessary for the triumph of evil is for good men to do nothing.[8]

Personalizing the Postcard

As the saying goes, one rotten apple spoils the whole barrel. But people in New Testament times used a different metaphor to describe the same idea: "A little leaven leavens the whole lump of dough" (Gal. 5:9). Leaven, or yeast, was used figuratively to refer to, among other things, the hypocrisy of the Pharisees (Luke 12:1), the teaching of the Pharisees and Sadducees (Matt. 16:12), and malice and wickedness (1 Cor. 5:8). Like yeast permeating dough, these covert forces of evil spread from small beginnings. Doctrinal and moral defection usually begin from almost imperceptible microbes of impurity. Contaminations like these are always easier to nip in the bacterial stage. Left to themselves, they can become a doughy mess virtually overnight. Is there a tiny, yeasty impurity lumped

---

5. Liddell and Scott, *A Greek-English Lexicon*, p. 1333.

6. Possibly under the guise of Paul's words in Romans 5:20—"where sin increased, grace abounded all the more"—these ungodly people took the license to liberate their lusts. Paul addressed this problem in Romans 6.

7. James Hope Moulton and George Milligan, *The Vocabulary of the Greek Testament* (Grand Rapids, Mich.: William B. Eerdmans Publishing Co., 1972), pp. 404–5.

8. Bartlett, *Familiar Quotations*, p. 454.

away and hidden somewhere in your life? Won't you deal with it now—before it spreads and makes a doughy mess of your life, your work, your relationships, your family, or your church?

 Living Insights

Study One ▬▬▬▬▬▬▬▬▬▬▬▬▬▬▬▬▬▬▬▬▬▬▬▬▬▬

As we come to our final postcard, let's continue the pattern we have established, and take an overall look at the letter of Jude.

- Copy the chart below into your notebook, and add your own titles and observations.

	OVERVIEW OF JUDE					
	Title:	Title:	Title:	Title:	Title:	Title:
SALUTATION	Observations:	Observations:	Observations:	Observations:	Observations:	Observations:
1–2	3–4	5–7	8–13	14–16	17–23	24–25

 Living Insights

Study Two ▬▬▬▬▬▬▬▬▬▬▬▬▬▬▬▬▬▬▬▬▬▬▬▬▬▬

Since we'll be going through the letter of Jude at a more relaxed pace, let's pause to consider the key thought of the first section—contending for the faith.

- Bring your family or friends together for a discussion. Use the following questions as "starters" to get everyone involved. Stay away from predictable answers by trying to express yourself in fresh terms.
  —In the phrase "contend earnestly for the faith," what is meant by the word *contend?*
  —How can "contending" be demonstrated today in your own set of circumstances?
  —What is "the faith"? What's involved in it? What's not involved?
  —In the past, have you contended for the faith in a proper or improper way?

Why Bother to Battle?

Jude 5–16

Published in 1891, Oscar Wilde's book *The Picture of Dorian Gray* is a tragic one. The story opens with an artist finishing a full-length portrait of an exquisitely handsome man named Dorian Gray, whose features are marked by innocence and purity. Dorian loves the artist's work but is disturbed because he realizes that the picture will remain eternally young while he himself will eventually become old and ugly. He declares that he would give his soul if only the portrait would age and he would remain perpetually young. In the following months, Dorian falls into bad company and a life of self-indulgent pleasures. After ruthlessly jilting a love-struck starlet, he returns home to find the portrait slightly changed. Although the mirror shows his features as fresh and innocent as ever, in the portrait a cruel grimace distorts his mouth. Dorian hides the portrait, terrified of revealing his true self. In the years that follow, Dorian satisfies every debauched desire. Each sin he commits causes the portrait to grow more and more grotesque. He becomes obsessed with comparing his youthful, unravaged face in the mirror with the cruel and gruesome one in the portrait. In a moment of tragic perception, he seizes a knife and passionately slashes the picture. When his servants hear an agonizing cry, they break down the locked door. Entering the room, they see the picture of Dorian Gray as it looked originally—innocent, pure, and compelling. But on the floor lies the true Dorian Gray who, in stabbing the portrait, has actually killed himself. Old, withered, and repulsive, he is unrecognizable to his own servants. A Dorian Gray portrait of false teachers emerges throughout Jude's postcard. Jude entreats his readers to beware—no matter what these teachers appear to be on the surface, they are hidden reefs of deception and destruction. And, like Dorian Gray, their doom is certain. In the title to this study, we ask the question, "Why Bother to Battle?" The answer lies in the portrait Jude paints of the apostates.

I. A Portrait of the Apostates

In the short twenty-five verses that comprise Jude, the author uses vivid images to portray the true character of the apostate teachers who "crept in unnoticed" and infiltrated the church: they are licentious (v. 4); they deny Jesus as their Lord and Master (v. 4); they "defile the flesh, and reject authority, and revile angelic majesties" (v. 8); they revile what they don't understand (v. 10); they are "hidden reefs ... clouds without water ... trees without fruit ... wild waves ... wandering stars" (vv. 12–13); they are grumblers, faultfinders, followers after their own lusts, arrogant, and seek for their own gain by flattery (v. 16); they are divisive, worldly, and "devoid of the Spirit" (v. 19). Regardless how smooth their words or enticing their teaching, their true character, like Dorian Gray's, has turned grotesquely evil and repugnant. We bother to battle not only because the evil is so great but because it is so deceptive and destructive.

II. A Bold Reminder

In exhorting us to contend for the faith, Jude gives some bold reminders concerning apostates.

A. Their doom is certain. Turning back the pages of time, Jude dusts off three examples from the annals of history to assure us that the doom of apostates is inevitable:

> Now I desire to remind you, though you know all things once for all, that the Lord, after saving a people out of the land of Egypt, subsequently destroyed those who did not believe. And angels who did not keep their own domain, but abandoned their proper abode, He has kept in eternal bonds under darkness for the judgment of the great day. Just as Sodom and Gomorrah and the cities around them, since they in the same way as these indulged in gross immorality and went after strange flesh, are exhibited as an example, in undergoing the punishment of eternal fire. (vv. 5–7)

Jude's first example (v. 5) is an incident from the history of Israel recorded in Numbers 13–14. This is the dreadful reminder of those Israelites who were led out of Egypt, traveled across the desert, and arrived at the very borders of the Promised Land. But because of unbelief, they experienced death in the wilderness rather than rest in the land of milk and honey. It is this wilderness graveyard that not only haunts the minds of Paul and the writer to the Hebrews (1 Cor. 10:5–11, Heb. 3:18–4:2) but looms forebodingly in Jude's thinking as well.

An Example and Exhortation

In Hebrews 3:18–19, we read that Israel was prevented from entering into God's rest because of unbelief. In 4:1, we are exhorted to fear lest the same fate befall *us*. In summary form, 1 Corinthians 10:1–12 recounts Israel's wilderness experience, with the last two verses closing in an exhortation:

> Now these things happened to them as an example, and they were written for our instruction, upon whom the ends of the ages have come. Therefore let him who thinks he stands take heed lest he fall.

> Each step we take in our walk with Christ can be the
> beginning of a fall—unless, of course, His truth is the
> ground upon which we walk. Be careful *where* you step
> and *how* you step; only Christ is the solid Rock. Where are
> you walking, theologically and morally, at this time in your
> life? Where do you stand? On solid rock or sinking sand?

In Jude's second example (v. 6), the scene changes from the
world of men to that of angels. Jude describes the judgment of
the angels in Genesis 6:1–4, when they broke rank and stepped
lustfully beyond their prescribed abode to cohabit with human
women. In his third example (v. 7), Jude recalls to our minds
the destruction of the wicked cities of Sodom and Gomorrah
(see Gen. 18–19). Like those rebellious angels, the apostates
"crept in unnoticed," impregnating the church with their lies
and licentiousness. And like the fallen angels, the unbelieving
Israelites, and the immoral inhabitants of Sodom and Gomorrah,
their destruction would be swift and certain.

┌─ *A Lesson from History* ─────────────────────────────
If you are defecting from Jesus, denying Him as Master and
Lord over both your mind and morals, remember: God
does not show partiality (Rom. 2:11). As He punished the
wicked people of Sodom and Gomorrah, so He disciplined
unbelieving Israel—"the apple of His eye" (Zech. 2:8). And
as He punished men who sinned, so He punished angels,
who, before defecting, once sang His praises.

B. Their tongues are blasphemous. Jesus says: " 'The good
man out of the good treasure of his heart brings forth what is
good; and the evil man out of the evil treasure brings forth what
is evil; for his mouth speaks from that which fills his heart' "
(Luke 6:45). In verses 8–10, Jude recounts the revilings of these
apostates, and from their verbal attacks, their true nature is
revealed:

> Yet in the same manner these men, also by dreaming,
> defile the flesh, and reject authority, and revile an-
> gelic majesties. But Michael the archangel, when he
> disputed with the devil and argued about the body
> of Moses, did not dare pronounce against him a rail-
> ing judgment, but said, "The Lord rebuke you." But
> these men revile the things which they do not under-
> stand; and the things which they know by instinct,

like unreasoning animals, by these things they are destroyed.

The words *angelic majesties* in verse 8 literally mean "glories." As the people of Sodom and Gomorrah defiled the flesh, so did the apostates. As the fallen angels rebelled and broke rank, so the apostates rejected authority. And as the Israelites reviled Moses and Aaron—the brightest luminaries in the nation's hierarchy—so these men reviled the highest teachers and teachings within the church. Verse 9, by contrast, indicates the total irreverence of their blasphemous revilings. Even the archangel Michael did not dare speak out against Satan, the leader of evil angels.[1] But these men, the apostates, speak indignantly of divine things, charging in boldly where angels fear to tread. One characteristic of apostates is their cynical irreverence toward things that are sacred and holy. A second grotesque characteristic is their verbal reviling of things they don't understand. What they do understand, however, is their own animal instincts. Their way of life is to allow the instincts they share with "unreasoning animals" to run wild in the streets—unleashed and unrestrained. The last clause in verse 10 shockingly reveals how this lifestyle, governed only by animal instincts, withers and disfigures character: "by these things they are destroyed [lit. corrupted]" (see Eph. 4:22).

C. Their religion is empty. These evil men are worth the bother to battle, not only because their doom is certain (vv. 5–7) and their words blasphemous (vv. 8–10), but because their religion is empty (vv. 11–13). Turning from examples of departures en masse from God's truth to individual ones, Jude informs us that apostasy is nothing new; it's as old as the human race.

> Woe to them! For they have gone the way of Cain,
> and for pay they have rushed headlong into the error
> of Balaam, and perished in the rebellion of Korah.
> (v. 11)

"The way of Cain" is the broad way that leads to destruction (Matt. 7:13–14). It's a religion that offers the fruit of man's works in order to gain acceptance with God rather than the innocent

---

1. The unusual story of Moses' death is told in Deuteronomy 34:1–6. However, here Jude cites an apocryphal book titled The Assumption of Moses. This work adds to the story in Deuteronomy by stating that the task of burying the body of Moses was given to the archangel Michael. Complicating his task, Satan laid claim to Moses' body. For an excellent discussion on this verse and why Satan disputed over Moses' body, see *Jude: The Acts of the Apostates* by S. Maxwell Coder (Chicago, Ill.: Moody Press, 1958), pp. 58–63.

blood of a substitutionary sacrifice.[2] In a word, this religion is *empty*. "The error of Balaam" refers to the teaching and treachery of an Old Testament prophet whose allegiance, like that of Judas Iscariot, could be bought.[3] He was a prophet greedy for gold, whose life epitomized the sacrifice of eternal riches for temporal ones. Balaam's error was his compelling and consuming desire to gain some part of the world—even at the loss of his soul (see Mark 8:36). Except for the coins in Balaam's purse, his religion had an empty ring to it. Like Balaam and Dorian Gray, the apostates have bartered away their souls. Finally, their deeds are compared to "the rebellion of Korah." Korah was a Levite and cousin to Moses (Exod. 6:18–21). Under Korah's leadership, a cauldron of rebellion began to boil against the authority of Moses and Aaron. Korah had dared to think that "all the congregation [was] holy" (Num. 16:3) and presumed he could approach a holy God without Moses and Aaron, God's chosen mediators. Because of his defiance, he and his followers were swallowed up in an earthquake of judgment from the Lord (Num. 16:31–33). Korah's religion, too, was empty—empty of authority.

Reflections on Apostasy

Verse 11 glistens with reflections concerning apostasy. First, it is not confined to one class of people. Cain was a tiller of the soil; Balaam was a prophet; Korah was a Levite. It affects not only leaders but lay people as well. Second, apostasy is a progression. Notice the steep, downhill slide: "They have gone . . . , rushed headlong . . . , and perished." The words are reminiscent of those in Mark 5:12–13, where demons "entered the swine . . . rushed down the steep bank . . . and they were drowned in the sea." Third, apostasy—no matter how reasonable its words or winsome its ways—is diametrically opposed to Christ. Instead of the *way* of Christ, there is the way of Cain. Instead of the *truth* of Christ, there is the error of Balaam. Instead of the *life* of Christ, there is the death of Korah.

In a montage of images, Jude overlaps successive pictures of the apostates, each pregnant with meaning:

These men are those who are hidden reefs in your
love feasts when they feast with you without fear,

2. Compare Genesis 4:1–7 and Hebrews 11:4, 9:22.
3. Compare Numbers 22–24, Deuteronomy 23:4, Nehemiah 13:2, 2 Peter 2:15, and Revelation 2:14.

caring for themselves; clouds without water, carried along by winds; autumn trees without fruit, doubly dead, uprooted; wild waves of the sea, casting up their own shame like foam; wandering stars, for whom the black darkness has been reserved forever. (vv. 12–13)

Viewed together, these vivid pictures bring to life the character sketch of these false teachers. They are as deceptive as hidden reefs, as disappointing as clouds without water, as dead as trees that are without fruit and uprooted, as destructive as wild waves of the sea, and as doomed as falling stars.

D. Their ways are godless. Quoting Enoch,[4] an obscure prophet in Israel's history whose writings are preserved outside the canon of Scripture, Jude now launches the most frontal attack in his battle against the apostate teachers:

And about these also Enoch, in the seventh generation from Adam, prophesied, saying, "Behold, the Lord came with many thousands of His holy ones, to execute judgment upon all, and to convict all the ungodly of all their ungodly deeds which they have done in an ungodly way, and of all the harsh things which ungodly sinners have spoken against Him. These are grumblers, finding fault, following after their own lusts; they speak arrogantly, flattering people for the sake of gaining an advantage. (vv. 14–16)

As Jude puts aside his palette, and the paint of these verses begins to dry, we can take a step back and get a full view of this portrait: we see the lips sneering contemptuously in complaint, a faultfinding finger pointed in ridicule, eyes glinting with lust, an eyebrow lifted in arrogance, the appearance of a manipulative flatterer. We see Dorian Gray as we look at this portrait of the apostate—grotesque and repulsive.

---

4. One of the unusual things about Jude is that he takes his quotations not only from Scripture but from the apocryphal books as well—that is, from books not in the Old Testament. These works of literature were popular and widely used in Jude's time, so to his readers, the quotations would have been extremely effective. The practice of quoting noncanonical literature raises a red flag in some people's minds. However, it is no different from a preacher using quotations in his sermon that are not from the Bible. Both Stephen (in Acts 7) and Jesus (in Matt. 23) refer to historical incidents not mentioned in the Old Testament. Even a pagan work could contain elements of truth, as Paul attests when he quotes the poet Aratus's *Phaenomena 5* to his educated Athenian audience in Acts 17:28. For further discussion, see *Encyclopedia of Bible Difficulties* by Gleason L. Archer (Grand Rapids, Mich.: Zondervan Publishing House, 1982), p. 430.

III. A Cautioned Strategy

We can't help but feel like lashing out at the evil portrayed in the picture of the apostate. Before we do, however, we need to know where we stand and where our enemy stands. We need to search the Scriptures consistently, so we'll be unafraid of standing alone in the battle.

A Final Application

There is a difference between contending for the faith and simply being *contentious*. The former is frontline fighting with the enemy; the latter, back-stabbing behind the lines within our own troops. The one we are commanded to do (Jude 3); the other, to avoid (Titus 3:9).

Living Insights

Study One

The passage we have studied contains a careful and colorful description of the false teachers. It was important to expose their traits in order to recognize them easily.

● There's a remarkable similarity between the description of false teachers by Jude and the one given by Peter in his second letter. Let's do a comparative study of the two texts. Copy the chart below into your notebook, and jot down observations on both passages. Notice the similarities between the two descriptions.

Characteristics of the False Teachers	
Jude 5–16	2 Peter 2:1–22

Continued on next page

🌹 Living Insights

Fighting a spiritual battle is neither glamorous nor enjoyable. But Jude tells us that it is necessary. This means we must be prepared, by knowing both *where we stand* and *where our enemy stands.*

- Where do you stand on some of the "essentials" of Christianity? Pinpoint your position in each of the following categories by writing a paragraph that expresses it.
  —The Bible
  —The Trinity
  —Jesus Christ
  —Salvation
- Where does the enemy stand on these issues? Summarize what you know of the enemy in each category.
  —The Bible
  —The Trinity
  —Jesus Christ
  —Salvation

⚒ Digging Deeper

The interpretation of Jude 6 has resulted in a babel of commentators. However, it appears to be an echo of Genesis 6. Work through the following points to see how we arrived at this conclusion. First, the Bible commonly used at the time Jude was writing was a Greek translation of the Old Testament known as the Septuagint. In that version, the phrase "sons of God" in Genesis 6:2 and 4 is translated "angels of God." Second, support for this translation can be found in Job 1:6, 2:1, and 38:7, where the phrase "sons of God" can only refer to angels. In these passages, the Septuagint also translates the phrase as "angels of God." Third, the context of Genesis 6:2 and 4 favors this interpretation. There was something strange and terrible in the unholy unions described in this passage—something much more serious than godly men taking ungodly wives. Obviously, it was a problem of potentially catastrophic proportions. Why else would God have resorted to such a catastrophic remedy as a worldwide flood? Fourth, the context of Jude 7 favors this interpretation. The people of Sodom and Gomorrah are said to have gone after strange flesh, "in the same way as these indulged in gross immorality." Fifth, the broader context of the New Testament seems to support this view as well (2 Pet. 2:4). Extrabiblical literature from Jude's time also supports this view. Sixth, the apocryphal book of Enoch, from which Jude quotes and to which he alludes, refers to a similar fall of angelic beings. Josephus, a great Jewish historian and contemporary of Jude, notes: "Many angels accompanied with women, and begat sons that proved unjust" (*Antiquities* 1:3:1). For support of this interpretation, see *A Commentary on the Book of Genesis* by Umberto Cassuto (Jerusalem: The Magnes Press, 1961), vol. 1, pp. 290–301. Also, *Biblical Demonology* by Merrill F. Unger (Wheaton, Ill.: Scripture Press, 1952), pp. 17–19, 45–52. For other interpretations, see *The Pentateuch*, vol. 1 of Commentary on the Old Testament in Ten Volumes by C. F. Keil and F. Delitzsch (Grand Rapids, Mich.: William B. Eerdmans Publishing Co., 1965), pp. 127–138. See also, "Divine Kingship and Genesis 6:1–4" by Meredith G. Kline, *Westminster Theological Journal* (Nov. 1961–May 1962), p. 197.

Get Your Act Together
Jude 17–25

As the war against Hitler raged in Europe, Sir Winston Churchill, in his first statement as prime minister, addressed the House of Commons on May 13, 1940, with these words:

I have nothing to offer but blood, toil, tears and sweat.[1]

Speaking again to the House of Commons on June 4, 1940, about the evacuation of the Allied forces at Dunkirk, this tenacious bulldog of the British Empire stood his ground with this stirring speech:

We shall not flag or fail. We shall go on to the end. We shall fight in France, we shall fight on the seas and oceans, we shall fight with growing confidence and growing strength in the air, we shall defend our island, whatever the cost may be, we shall fight on the beaches, we shall fight on the landing grounds, we shall fight in the fields and in the streets, we shall fight in the hills; we shall never surrender.[2]

Churchill's words flow with the fixed resolve of a man contending earnestly for the preservation of his country. With similar determination, Jude exhorts us to "contend earnestly for the faith" (v. 3). The enemy here is apostasy; what hangs in the balance is the preservation of truth and morality. In verses 17–25, Jude makes a final appeal to the soldiers of the faith who are in the midst of a raging battle against the onslaught of apostasy.

I. Final Instructions for the Troops

In the remainder of this postcard, Jude takes the cross hairs of his gun sights off the enemy, puts his weapon down, and addresses his troops.

A. Remember the training manual. With the phrase "but you, beloved," Jude changes subjects from the grumbling, fault-finding, arrogant, flattering words of the apostates (v. 16) to the words of the apostles.

But you, beloved, ought to remember the words that were spoken beforehand by the apostles of our Lord Jesus Christ, that they were saying to you, "In the last time there shall be mockers, following after their own ungodly lusts." These are the ones who cause divisions, worldly-minded, devoid of the Spirit. (vv. 17–19)

---

1. Sir Winston Spencer Churchill in *Bartlett's Familiar Quotations,* 14th ed. (Boston, Mass.: Little, Brown and Co., 1968), p. 920.

2. Bartlett, *Familiar Quotations,* p. 921.

The apostles' words[3] alert the troops to a timetable in God's battle plans so that the sudden assault of the apostates won't take them by surprise. The infiltration of mockers who follow after their own ungodly lusts comes with the territory of the last times. In defending the borders of the faith, we are to keep a vigilant watch with our binoculars, scanning the horizon for enemy movement. The apostles teach us how to pierce the enemy's camouflage. Listen to their words and look at their lifestyle; when you see mockers with loose morals, be on the alert. Besides their conversations and conduct, another identifying trait is listed in verse 19: "These are the ones who cause divisions." Wherever they go, friendships falter, strife surfaces, and congregations crumble. They don't bring unity, which is a characteristic of the Spirit and of those in close fellowship with Christ (1 Cor. 12:12–13, John 17:22–23). There is a telling reason why unity does not characterize their relationships: they are "devoid of the Spirit." Is it any wonder that their motivations and methods are "worldly-minded" or humanistic?

Belief and Behavior

Turning away from God's Word is the defiant first step toward apostasy. It also marks the beginning of eroding morals. Denial of Jesus as "Master and Lord" and licentiousness are linked together in verse 4. Saying harsh things against the Lord and performing ungodly deeds are closely associated in verse 15. Mocking authority and following after ungodly lusts seem to go hand in hand in verse 18. One by one, the rocks that form the pinnacles of our character break loose. As they tumble down the steep slopes of compromise and shatter to pieces, an avalanche of immorality results. Is your life losing ground in a washout of morals? The first step in character conservation is a step back into God's Word: "The law of the Lord is perfect, *restoring* the soul" (Ps. 19:7, emphasis added).

B. Keep in shape. Jude was concerned not only with the apostate teachers who were battering the gates of the Christian faith, but he was also concerned with the well-being of his soldiers standing watch on the walls:

> But you, beloved, building yourselves up on your
> most holy faith; praying in the Holy Spirit; keep

---

3. See 2 Peter 3:3, Acts 20:29, 1 Timothy 4:1, and 2 Timothy 3:1–5.

yourselves in the love of God, waiting anxiously for
the mercy of our Lord Jesus Christ to eternal life.
(vv. 20–21)

The imperative is to "keep yourselves in the love of God" (v. 21).
The clauses surrounding this main command describe how it is
done—by "building yourselves up...praying...waiting anxiously." In military terms, Jude is exhorting the troops to readiness. They are to stay in shape, keep in close communication
with headquarters, and watch vigilantly for the coming of their
Commander in Chief. In his speech to the Canadian Senate and
House of Commons on December 30, 1941, Churchill voiced
similar sentiments on the necessity of soldiers to be not only
willing but able:

In this strange, terrible world war there is a place for
everyone, man and woman, old and young, hale and
halt; service in a thousand forms is open. There is
no room now for the dilettante, the weakling, for the
shirker, or the sluggard.[4]

As wartime demands peak readiness in the physical realm, to
"contend earnestly for the faith" demands peak readiness in the
spiritual realm.

Battle Stations

Praying in the Holy Spirit is first an admission of our
weakness. The Lord tells us "as the heavens are higher
than the earth, / So are My ways higher than your ways, /
And My thoughts than your thoughts" (Isa. 55:9). Because
God is limitless and we are limited, there are often
communication gaps when we pray. The Holy Spirit
bridges these gaps when "He intercedes for the saints
according to the will of God" (Rom. 8:26–27). When we
acknowledge our weakness, depend on the Holy Spirit to
bridge this gap, and have a spirit submissive to God's
will—whatever that may prove to be—we are praying *in
the Spirit* (see Luke 22:41–42). God's thoughts will then
become our thoughts and His ways, our ways. Praying in
the Spirit brings both clarity and courage. We are never so
strong as when we are in prayer. Kneeling knees don't
knock!

C. Rescue the war-torn. Lest the goal of the believer get
distorted in the preparation for war or in the heat of battle, Jude

---

4. Bartlett, *Familiar Quotations*, p. 923.

reminds the troops that the objective is not to win arguments but to win *people:*

> And have mercy on some, who are doubting; save others, snatching them out of the fire; and on some have mercy with fear, hating even the garment polluted by the flesh. (vv. 22–23)

We are to confront[5] those who doubt, or convince them by patient instruction (1 Pet. 3:15, Eph. 4:15). Verse 23 indicates we are to save others by "snatching them out of the fire." Flirting with falsehood is playing with fire. When we reach out to those engulfed in the flames of apostasy, we may grab them uncomfortably by the scruff of their necks, but we will save their lives from certain destruction (see James 5:19–20). The second half of verse 23 tells us how to approach people in need: mercifully and "with fear." There is always certain danger for the sinner, but there is also the risk of danger to the rescuer. A physician who reaches out to cure a disease-ridden patient always runs the risk of infection. Jude warns that we must approach the infected person cautiously, "hating even the garment polluted by the flesh."[6] We are to have mercy, while hating everything having to do with the sin of the guilty—even down to their inner garment, which is a symbol of all that touches or surrounds the sinner. As the garment is stained and spotted by dirt, so the atmosphere surrounding the sinner is polluted. We are to love sinners and approach them mercifully, but we must hate the atmosphere, the environment, and the alluring garments in which sin is sometimes clothed.

II. Final Benediction for the Troops

You can almost see the troops gathered around the platform where Jude, a prime minister of the early church, is concluding his speech. Hanging on his every word, the troops listen intently. There is no shuffling among the ranks . . . no whispers. They wait silently as he raises his arms to bless them. In the rhetoric of a Churchill, he pronounces the final, stirring benediction before the battle.

> Now to Him who is able to keep you from stumbling,[7] and to make you stand in the presence of His glory

---

5. The Greek text of verse 22 is uncertain. Some manuscripts read "mercy," while others read "confront" or "convince." The latter seems more likely.

6. Almost certainly, Jude is thinking here of the regulations in Leviticus 13:47–52.

7. The word *stumbling* is translated from the Greek word *aptaistos.* It is used in a literal sense to describe a surefooted horse that does not stumble. In a metaphorical sense, it refers to a good man who does not fall into error or sin. See Psalms 66:9 and 121:3.

blameless[8] with great joy, to the only God our Savior, through Jesus Christ our Lord, be glory, majesty, dominion and authority, before all time and now and forever. Amen. (vv. 24–25)

In a crescendo of emotion inspired by verse 25, Jude fans the embers within their hearts and enflames their souls with a consuming loyalty to the Lord and Savior they serve. He dismisses them with a simple, quiet amen. As they march away steadfastly, to face the opposition within the church and the persecution from without, surely the "angelic majesties" looked down upon them and said: "This was their finest hour."[9]

Living Insights

Study One

Not only does Jude cover the characteristics of apostates, but he also includes a strategy believers can use to achieve victory.

- Jude 17–25 is brimming with helpful suggestions for us as believers. In your own words, paraphrase the verses that apply to Christians today. In light of the forces and factions that threaten the Church, how would you apply Jude's exhortation to "contend earnestly for the faith"?

Living Insights

Study Two

As a result of our study, do you feel more comfortable with these postcards from the New Testament? Let's use our final time together to review the high points.

- Go back over your notes from this series. Copy the chart below into your notebook. Write in the most significant truths you learned and the most appropriate applications.

Letters	Truths	Applications
Philemon		
2 John		
3 John		
Jude		

8. The Greek word for "blameless" is *amōmos*. It is used of an animal that was without spot or blemish, and therefore acceptable as a sacrifice to God.

9. Bartlett, *Familiar Quotations*, p. 921.

Books for Probing Further

Before you bundle up these postcards with a rubber band and tuck them away, thumb through them one final time so the images make an imprint on your memory. Philemon pictures a runaway slave appealing to his former owner for forgiveness. Second John reveals a woman who was so eager to be hospitable that she ended up giving shelter to the enemy—the false teachers. Third John, on the other hand, cameos three men, one of whom made it a habit to rudely refuse hospitality to the *true* teachers of the church. Coming to the bottom of the stack, Jude unveils a true portrait of the false teachers, and in doing so, admonishes us to "contend earnestly for the faith."

These picture postcards come to us from halfway around the world and provide us with a revealing collage of the character of the first century church. But the ink on the postmarks is as fresh as if these postcards were sent yesterday, the pictures as vivid and unfaded as if they were taken last Sunday at a church picnic, and the applications as personal as if addressed to each of us individually.

Are there some postcards *you* need to write? Is there someone like Philemon you need to communicate with—to ask for forgiveness, to restore a severed relationship? Are you, like the lady in 2 John, naive about the kind of people you welcome into your home? Of course, with the modern convenience of hotels, we don't generally give room and board to itinerant preachers anymore. But perhaps, through the modern innovations of television and radio, you're letting the wrong type of people into your home. Perhaps you're aiding and abetting the enemy by listening to some misguided or false teachers, by receiving their literature, or by sending an occasional donation in support of their causes. If that's the case, maybe you need to drop a postcard of your own in the mail asking them to take you off their mailing list and informing them that they are no longer welcome in your home. Or perhaps, like Diotrephes in 3 John, you're on the other extreme. Maybe the door to your home stays dead-bolted, to the extent that the genuinely good and honest teachers of the gospel are turned away brusquely. If so, buy some invitations announcing an "open house," and unlatch the door to your heart and home. Let them know they are honored guests and that they are always welcome.

Like the apostates described by Jude, do you have hidden theological or moral corruption in your life that needs to be brought into the open? Whether it's in your own heart or in the halls of Congress, it needs to be addressed. You can "contend earnestly for the faith," as Jude exhorts, by dropping a note to your congressman, governor, mayor, or school superintendent. Encourage each one not only to stand up for biblical truth and values but also to apply them to their respective spheres of responsibility.

We've had an interesting and enjoyable time reading the incoming mail, *New Testament Postcards,* but now we need to look at the *outgoing* mail baskets on our desks. If yours is empty, I trust that God's Spirit will prompt you to write a few postcards of your own, that He will guide your words in love and in truth, and that they will be timely and well-received. Happy writing, and may all your letters be first class!

I. Philemon
Technical Commentary
Lightfoot, J. B. *Saint Paul's Epistles to the Colossians and to Philemon.* 1879. Reprint. Grand Rapids, Mich.: Zondervan Publishing House, 1957.
Nontechnical Commentary
Hiebert, D. Edmond. *Titus and Philemon.* Chicago, Ill.: Moody Press, 1957.

II. 2 John and 3 John
Technical Commentary
Marshall, I. Howard. *The Epistles of John.* Grand Rapids, Mich.: William B. Eerdmans Publishing Co., 1978.
Nontechnical Commentary
Coder, S. Maxwell. *Jude: The Acts of the Apostates.* Chicago, Ill.: Moody Press, 1958.

III. Jude
Technical Commentary
Mayor, Joseph B. *The Epistles of Jude and Second Peter.* Grand Rapids, Mich.: Baker Book House, 1965.
Nontechnical Commentary
Coder, S. Maxwell. *Jude: The Acts of the Apostates.* Chicago, Ill.: Moody Press, 1958.

IV. Doctrine
Technical Study
Thiessen, Henry Clarence. *Lectures in Systematic Theology.* Revised by Vernon D. Doerksen. Grand Rapids, Mich.: William B. Eerdmans Publishing Co., 1983.
Nontechnical Study
Swindoll, Charles R. *Growing Deep in the Christian Life.* Portland, Oreg.: Multnomah Press, 1986.

Insight for Living
Cassette Tapes
NEW TESTAMENT POSTCARDS

Do you like small packages covered in attractive wrappings? Then you will love these missiles of truth, each one no more than one chapter long. But talk about packing a wallop! Here are several powerful "postcards" that refuse to be ignored.

			U.S.	Canadian
NTP	CS	Cassette series—includes album cover	$18.75	$23.75
		Individual cassettes—include messages		
		A and B	5.00	6.35

These prices are effective as of September 1986 and are subject to change without notice.

NTP 1-A: ***A Postcard to Philemon***
Philemon
   B: ***A Postcard to a Lady and Her Kids***
2 John

NTP 2-A: ***A Postcard of Candid Truth***
3 John
   B: ***The Acts of the Apostates***
Jude 1–4

NTP 3-A: ***Why Bother to Battle?***
Jude 5–16
   B: ***Get Your Act Together!***
Jude 17–25

Ordering Information

U.S. ordering information: You are welcome to use our toll-free number (for Visa and MasterCard orders only) between the hours of 8:30 A.M. and 4:00 P.M., Pacific time, Monday through Friday. The number is **(800) 772-8888.** This number may be used anywhere in the continental United States excluding California, Hawaii, and Alaska. Orders from those areas are handled through our Sales Department at **(714) 870-9161.** We are unable to accept collect calls.

Your order will be processed promptly. We ask that you allow four to six weeks for delivery by fourth-class mail. If you wish your order to be shipped first-class, please add 10 percent of the total order cost (not including California sales tax) for shipping and handling.

Canadian ordering information: Your order will be processed promptly. We ask that you allow approximately four weeks for delivery by first-class mail to the U.S./Canadian border. All orders will be shipped from our office in Fullerton, California. For our listeners in British Columbia, a 7 percent sales tax must be added to the total of all tape orders (not including first-class postage). For further information, please contact our office at **(604) 272-5811.**

Payment options: We accept personal checks, money orders, Visa, and MasterCard in payment for materials ordered. Unfortunately, we are unable to offer invoicing or COD orders. If the amount of your check or money order is less than the amount of your purchase, your check will be returned so that you may place your order again with the correct amount. All orders must be paid in full before shipment can be made.

Returned checks: There is a $10 charge for any returned check (regardless of the amount of your order) to cover processing and invoicing.

Guarantee: Our tapes are guaranteed for ninety days against faulty performance or breakage due to a defect in the tape. For best results, please be sure your tape recorder is in good operating condition and is cleaned regularly.

Mail your order to one of the following addresses:

Insight for Living	Insight for Living Ministries
Sales Department	Post Office Box 2510
Post Office Box 4444	Vancouver, BC
Fullerton, CA 92634	Canada V6B 3W7

Quantity discounts and gift certificates are available upon request.

Overseas ordering information is provided on the reverse side of the order form.

Order Form

Please send me the following cassette tapes:

The current series: ☐ NTP CS New Testament Postcards
Individual cassettes: ☐ NTP 1 ☐ NTP 2 ☐ NTP 3

I am enclosing:

$ _____ To purchase the cassette series for $18.75 (in Canada $23.75*) which includes the album cover

$ _____ To purchase individual tapes at $5.00 each (in Canada $6.35*)

$ _____ Total of purchases

$ _____ If the order will be delivered in California, please add 6 percent sales tax

$ _____ U.S. residents please add 10 percent for first-class shipping and handling if desired

$ _____ *British Columbia residents please add 7 percent sales tax

$ _____ Canadian residents please add 6 percent for postage

$ _____ **Overseas residents please add appropriate postage** (See postage chart under "Overseas Ordering Information.")

$ _____ As a gift to the Insight for Living radio ministry for which a tax-deductible receipt will be issued

$ _____ **Total amount due (Please do not send cash.)**

Form of payment:

☐ Check or money order made payable to Insight for Living
☐ Credit card (Visa or MasterCard only)
If there is a balance: ☐ apply it as a donation ☐ please refund

---

Credit card purchases:
☐ Visa ☐ MasterCard number _____
Expiration date _____
Signature _____
We cannot process your credit card purchase without your signature.

Name _____

Address _____

_____

City _____

State/Province _____ Zip/Postal code _____

Country _____

Telephone (___) _____ Radio Station __ __ __ __

Should questions arise concerning your order, we may need to contact you.

Overseas Ordering Information

If you do not live in the United States or Canada, please note the following information. This will ensure efficient processing of your request.

Estimated time of delivery: We ask that you allow approximately twelve to sixteen weeks for delivery by surface mail. If you would like your order sent airmail, the length of delivery may be reduced. All orders will be shipped from our office in Fullerton, California.

Payment options: Due to fluctuating currency rates, we can accept only personal checks made payable in U.S. funds, international money orders, Visa, and MasterCard in payment for materials ordered. If the amount of your check or money order is less than the amount of your purchase, your check will be returned so that you may place your order again with the correct amount. All orders must be paid in full before shipment can be made.

Returned checks: There is a $10 charge for any returned check (regardless of the amount of your order) to cover processing and invoicing.

Postage and handling: Please add to the amount of purchase the postage cost for the service you desire. All orders must include postage based on the chart below.

Purchase Amount		Surface Postage	Airmail Postage
From	To	Percentage of Order	Percentage of Order
$ .01	$15.00	40%	75%
15.01	75.00	25%	45%
75.01	or more	15%	40%

Guarantee: Our tapes are guaranteed for ninety days against faulty performance or breakage due to a defect in the tape. For best results, please be sure your tape recorder is in good operating condition and is cleaned regularly.

Mail your order or inquiry to the following address:

Insight for Living
Sales Department
Post Office Box 4444
Fullerton, CA 92634

Quantity discounts and gift certificates are available upon request.